PAINTING THE PINWHEEL SKY

ANN HOWELLS

ASSURE PRESS

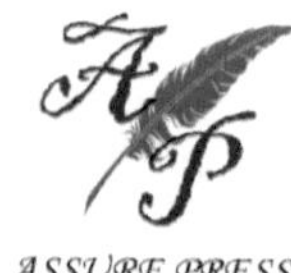

An imprint of Assure Press Publishing & Consulting, LLC

www.assurepress.org

Publisher's Note: Assure Press books may be purchased for educational, business, or sales promotional use. For information please visit the website.

Painting the Pinwheel Sky / Ann Howells. — 1st ed.

ISBN-13: 978-1-7335897-2-7
Library of Congress Control Number: 2020933084
eISBN-13: 978-1-7335897-3-4

These are persona poems, spoken primarily in the voice of Vincent Van Gogh and others who were prominent in his life. Italicized passages within the poems are direct quotations from Van Gogh's letters to his brother Theo. In other poems, Van Gogh's thoughts and ideas are frequently paraphrased, summarized, or interpreted. The epigrams attributed to VVG are also from Van Gogh's letters.

In several places, additional quotations are attributed, by name, to others, including the entire text of Emile Barnard's letter. All of these writings are in the public domain.

CONTENTS

PAINTING THE PINWHEEL SKY

Vincent Explains His Passion

> *I have played hell somewhat*
> *with the truthfulness of the colors.*
> -VVG

I resent hours wasted,
hence sleep poorly,
and I often eat at my easel,
though tales of eating paint
are exaggerated. More likely paint on lips
and chin result
from tongue-smoothing a brush,
wiping a brow with stained hand.
Marvel was most certainly correct: time
is a winged chariot. Hours and days fly:
too much world, too little time!
I even work at midday,
in full sunlight, with no shade at all,
in the cornfields,
and enjoy it all like a cicada.

In a certain way I am glad
that I have not learned painting.
I would bypass many lovely effects
in efforts to be correct. As it is,
my work evolves —
seven canvasses of sunflowers:
singly and arranged with roses, daisies,
other sunflowers.
I paint them again and again,
until I get them right —
not like a photograph, but a painting
that reveals,
exposes everything a sunflower holds:

flower and my reaction
exposed, explored, expressed! A paradigm!
But, perhaps, I am overwrought,
a madman,
dabbing and slashing paint.

Vincent Speaks of Theo

> *. . . now **I** say it less in words*
> *and more silently in work.*
> -VVG

Theo is my brother, my keeper,
patron and confessor,
strong right hand.
Dear Theo, takes me in,
battered suitcase beneath our bed,
extends the soup
with a handful of barley,
a cup of water.

Last year
I completed three landscapes
while living on milk, bread,
a few eggs, and chestnuts
stolen from a vendor
who chased me with curses.
Theo's francs go for linseed oil,
turpentine, pigments.
I gaze at sable brushes
as other men at Follies' nudes.
My lust is all consuming.

I wonder Theo has time
to concern himself
with my disastrous love affairs.
His middle-class world
cannot understand
the demi-monde in which
we artists exist:
where line between mistress

and madame, model
and prostitute, dancer
and whore, is razor thin
and fluid.

I am but a moon
circling Theo's earth,
yet oh, what scintillation
a moon provides.

Kee Recounts Her Experience

> *In an artist's life, death is perhaps*
> *not the most difficult thing.*
>
> -VVG

I knew him, of course, a cousin
lanky, loose-jointed
like poorly constructed scaffolding,
slinking along the outskirts
at family gatherings, an odd one,
argumentative
and given to bursts of inflamed rhetoric.
He seemed harmless enough
until I returned to Father's house
still in my widow's black
and given to periods of weeping.
I greeted him as I did others
who expressed condolences,
but he, both fierce and awkward, stayed,
ginger brows drawn with intensity
above blazing eyes. Twice I rejected
his offer of marriage,
but when I visited the market he was there,
selecting rutabagas and chestnuts.
If I called at the bookseller's he was there
browsing a volume on Michelangelo.
And should I pause for a cup of chocolate
he'd materialize at my table,
unwelcome apparition
proffering buttered croissants,
urging me to take a little sustenance.

I was of fragile disposition,
and his habit of appearing suddenly —

rather like a garden mole — in unlikely places
quite unnerved me, set me to trembling.
At the baker's, the butcher's,
even the dressmaker's, he lurked,
staring with eyes that blazed like embers.
Father spoke to him quite sternly.
But I was aghast, reduced to tears,
fled to my sister's
when, to demonstrate commitment,
he held his hand in the lantern flame.

Congregation Leaving the Reformed Church in Nuenen ~ *1884-5*

> *. . . those very incorrectnesses, those deviations,*
> *remodellings, changes in reality . . . untruth*
> *if you like — but more true than the literal truth.*
> -VVG

I've sketched multiple studies of this small church
where Father preached. In each,
a gravedigger leans on heart-shaped spade
beyond the doors.
Were I to leave that loitering workman,
Mother would find rebuke, recrimination,
recall childhood accusations:
my name, my date, simply transferred
from a stillborn brother,
and I wish this gift to please Mother,
bedridden with fractured thighbone.
To appease her sensibilities
I over-paint a small congregation retiring,
dab in autumn foliage of which she is so fond,
but retain the dark heavy line of Japanese prints
so appropriate to that austere little building
without icon, fresco, or stained glass.
I paint it desolate, clinging to sere grass —
discarded box in desiccated landscape —
still, it will please her.

The Potato Eaters ~ 1885

> *Art is to console those who are broken*
> *by life.*
>
> -VVG

Neighborhood children chide,
dance about me in circles,
label me Rainbow Man,
for smeared and spattered hues adorning fabric
and flesh,
but they include me in their games.
Unable to afford a studio,
I set my easel near my pallet — cheap rent
and satisfactory light.
I eat from crockery in which I mix paint,
sometimes eat the paint itself
rather than pause my work.

Today, I paint potato eaters,
miners gathered in dim lamplight,
sustaining themselves on roots as I am sustained
by obsession:
roughhewn hands, knotted and stained, scabrous,
accustomed to honest labor.
I scowl at my own uncalloused ones.
Guilt drives me. Honest labor all there is.
Work and faith. Breath and passion.

Vincent in Love

I put my heart and my soul into my work,
and I have lost my mind in the process.
                              -VVG

They whisper that I'm crazy
to paint the stars as pinwheels,
churning ocean of sky,
houses askew, listing at crazy angles,
but it's my heart that's tipped,
not my eyes, my brain. I'm in love.
Marguerite, *la petite serveuse,*
way she leans in, pours *vin ordinaire,*
breasts creamy, round as honeydew,
small smile when I stare,
upward glance through lashes,
flashes stockinged ankle as she strolls away.
She simply flirts, I know,
and what use has she for a melancholy painter.
Yet, I am drunk on love
and wine, *pirouette* this muddied street
as though it were *Rue de Madeleine,*
and every house and every tree whorls
and spins with me, stretches
toward the ever-whirling, ever-taunting stars.

He Called Me Sien

If the storm within gets too loud
I take a glass too much to stun myself.
                                    -VVG

If I give him clap he deserved it,
coulda got it anywhere —
he likes his whores!
Called me "mistress" and "model"
jus' means him sketchin' me all hours —
mendin' a skirt, combin' my hair —
no peace!
Pissin' away Theo's francs on paint
while I sold my ass for food,
screwin' me to the mattress.

Some say I owe him? Crap!
Takin' me in, they say,
knocked up whore, they say,
and draggin' a twelve-year-old.
What do they know! Sure I drink,
need my good times, him too —
absinthe if we got, but whatever —
I seen him guzzle turpentine
my gut won't handle.
Fightin' screamin' tossin' canvasses,
him cussin' paintin', rantin',
swearin' he'd never git it right.
I cussed him good,
he'd rant, eat paint,
mutter under his breath.
Kids pulled blankets on their heads,
and next door called the cops.
Self-righteous assholes!

Sometimes though . . . sometimes
we'd drink absinthe, sing,
and in the morning he'd paint me
pulling on my stockings.

Vincent Paints a Self-Portrait

*It is difficult to know oneself, but
it isn't easy to paint oneself either.*
                              -VVG

Is this the visage I present to the world,
unkempt scarecrow?
Wild ginger hair a hasty haystack?
Wheat field following a storm?
Stubby beard the ass end of a billy goat?
No wonder children flee.
Mothers warn: *Don't go near the madman.*
He devours children like croissants and jam.
And perhaps it will come to that —
galleries and patrons look askance at my work,
toss me summarily curbside amid canvas clatter.
The wolf, voracious creature,
perpetually pounds my door;
several times he would have slipped inside
were it not for Theo. *Dieu bénisse, Theo.*
My gaunt frame would collapse upon itself
without him.
Still, I paint light-headed, tremble with hunger,
find nourishment only in my art,
inhale paint fume like savory stew,
splash skies in ever-darkening wild rivers
upon my canvas.
Steeples tilt at venomous wheeling stars.

The Red Vineyard ~ 1888

> *. . . in a painter's life: success is about
> the worst thing that can happen.*
>   -VVG

I'd only to close my eyes,
and the panorama returned:
lowering sun washing fields in amber,
ochre, saffron, globes of grapes aglow,
leaves browned and curling at edges —
think cadmium, think cochineal.
And the women, round shouldered
bent to their task, blue of skirts and scarves,
sunburned faces, stained hands,
the entire vista tinted as though
through a glass of wine, vibrant color
so real. I dabbed and streaked, stormed
as the landscape revealed itself on canvas
just as it appeared behind my burning lids,
emblazoned on my skull's interior,
The Red Vineyard.

When Theo arranged a Brussels show,
it sold. It sold.

Madame Agostina Voices Her Amusement

*It is better to be high-spirited even though
one makes more mistakes, than to be narrow-minded
and all prudent.*

-VVG

Ach, the family finds me unsuitable,
fears I seek a husband. Laughable!
My cafe is profitable. What need have I
for a man? Any man?
No, no, no! I seek only a companion,
someone as outrageous as myself,
who makes absurd pronouncements
and argues vociferously.

With Vincent at my side we are invited
to soirees and salons, lionized.
Our passions burn
so high, how can they not burn out?
This affair could never be sustained!
I could never
tolerate his contentiousness
on a permanent basis.
I could explain this to his family,
brows creased with worry,
mouths filled with mumbled cautions,
who fritter life away fretting
over what may or may not occur?
Life is a carnival, and I intend
to relish every ride!
My enterprise, his painting,
these are our true loves.

Cafe Terrace At Night ~ 1888

> *It amuses me enormously to paint the night*
> *right on the spot.*
>
> -VVG

Night suits me well,
Arles still,
quiet, no one to taunt,
mock in sing-song rhyme.
When money is scarce,
sulfur, and a bit of cobalt
are cheap
and readily available.

I paint in light spilling
from a *patisserie*
where bakers' buttered fingers
pat dough for *pain au chocolat.*
See how lines draw the eye
down the walkway
as though the viewer
is strolling.
I want him to feel it as I do:
the serenity,
the loneliness.

Occasionally *une fille de rue*
brings me to a rented room,
exchanges favors for a portrait —
insults both portrait
and painter
as she tosses me from her door.
That doesn't matter;

just look,
stars blaze like far off bonfires.

Vincent Dreams *Irises ~ 1889*

> *I dream my paintings, then I paint*
> *my dreams.*
>
> -VVG

Effulgence bursts from cut-crystal.
Coddled in their bifurcated sleeve
they are not quite blue
neither are they purple.
In their minds they are orchids
birth daughters from their roots
in humus-rich Southern soil
hold the future in cupped hands.
I am a scarecrow twirling my brush:
colors whorl, petals unfurl –
flaunt ruffled frill and fall
in interplay of tint and hue.
I hear their taffeta secrets:
perfumed hyacinths dismissed as harlots.
Lilies? My Dear, didn't you know?
Nothing but common wildflowers!
A red-headed madman, I toss in sleep;
my little yellow house at Arles
tilts awkwardly askew. Iris
spin like blazing meteors.

Session with Dr. Gachet

> *If I were to think of and dwell on*
> *disastrous possibilities, I could do nothing.*
>
> -VVG

I am, I fear, a failure,
always second best, a replacement,
named for a brother
stillborn a year before,
my name and date carved on that small stone,
where Mother wept each Sunday after church.

Off to boarding school — younger,
smaller, butt of jokes, victim of pranks,
it foreshadowed my entire life.
I'm destined, I know,
to lie in an unremarkable grave, mourned by few,
ignored by the world.

Expelled from seminary —
for rejecting Latin, of all things.
Ha. They failed to see the irony:
life everlasting offered in a dead language.

At the Belgian Church I worked among miners,
a posting no one wanted. Honest workmen:
bent, weary, with calloused hands
and coal grime staining their skins.
Christ of the Coal Mines they called me —
until the committee cancelled my contract.

Theo, alone, loves me,
but he has married. Where shall I turn
when he deserts me? What shall I do then?

Fired from the gallery, outsider at The Hague:
excluded from discussions,
the one show I did secure, a flop.
Galleries toss me out the door,
and every woman I've loved rebuffed me.
But when I paint I forget to eat, to sleep,
forget my failures —
there is just glorious, vibrant color
to suckle and sustain me, make me alive.

Therein lies the road to madness.

Portrait of Dr. Gachet ~ 1890

> *Ah! Portraiture, portraiture with the thought,*
> *the soul of the model in it, that is what I think*
> *must come.*

-VVG

Critics say I painted him to look like me,
and why should I not?
We're bound one to the other
by mercurial moods, by melancholia and obsessions.
By physical similarities and addictions.
Our spirits align:
I find myself in him and he in me.
How can I not, when I lift my brush, confuse us?
His threadbare coat, his angular, loose-jointed bones,
his manic or lethargic manner?
And I cannot resist dabbing a sprig of foxglove
at his right hand,
for he makes of it an elixir, strives to cure me.

His large house is filled with life:
two half-grown sons, dogs, cats, rabbits, ducks,
pigeons, even a goat and a strutting peacock.
How he thinks, I cannot imagine, but he does,
and deeply. He believes strongly in socialism,
in free love, and in cremation. He requests
friends donate hearts and even brains for study.
He made such a request of me,
but did not pressure when I declined.
He poses for me, and I gift him with a portrait.

He seeks, also, a place where I might find peace,
the asylum, *Saint-Remy-de-Provence,*

released mornings, to paint, at home evenings —
a lost sheep returned to the fold.
He is both doctor and friend —
I haven't many.

Almond Blossom ~ 1890

> *. . . and the paintings appear as in a dream.*
>   -VVG

How glad I was when Theo's letter arrived!
And while I truly would have preferred
they name the boy after Father,
like Theo himself,
now that naming is done, I will paint a picture for him,
something they can hang in the bedroom.

I am immediately drawn to the fruit trees
blooming mid-March:
apricot, peach, and plum. I paint them often,
but this painting . . . this painting will be
like no other,
a gift for my nephew, little Vincent.
I will utilize a muted palette: sepia, pink, green,
and, perhaps, turquoise.
I will paint the painting I have dreamed —
a close-up, floral study:
white almond blossoms and slender branches
against blue sky.

It cries out for delicate Impressionist strokes,
airiness achieved
with little paint on the brush,
Divisionism's dabbed color
for surface sparkle. And, yes, a branch
in the foreground, accessible, appearing to extend
beyond the frame, one single branch
to represent the entire tree.
Contour and placement, gnarls and twists

reminiscent of arrangements in Japanese prints —
light in Arles is very like light in Japan.

Ah, I am a fanatic I know,
but this painting burns a fire within me.

Vincent Finds Another Sister

> *. . . in fighting the difficulties the inmost*
> *strength of the heart is developed.*
>
> -VVG

When Theo wrote
of his impending marriage, I feared
that with a wife upon whom to lavish
his attention, his love, his money,
I would become a mere annoyance,
an obstacle.
But my fears were unfounded.
I have, in Johanna, another sister,
lovely, innocent and gentle in her ways.
She is a teacher, intelligent,
and shares Theo's enthusiasm for my art,
for my vision.
She is an advocate, a sisterly storm,
and now she is with child.

Theo's frequent letters,
and Johanna's postscripts,
exude optimism and future plans.
I am to visit
when the child arrives.
I do not believe it will be a girl,
for Theo's neighbor
placed hands on Johanna's abdomen
in the seventh month,
predicted a boy.
She has been right more often than not.
So there will be a young Theo
to perpetuate the Van Gogh name.

I will be an uncle;
my little family grows.

Loving and Losing

> *. . . impossible and highly unsuitable*
> *love affairs from which, as a rule, I emerge*
> *only with shame and disgrace.*
>
> -VVG

I despair of finding a wife,
know I am not a handsome man,
but homelier men than I have married.
Poorer men than I. What is it I lack?
Stability? Temperance? Charm?

Caroline, Eugénie just a year later,
perhaps I was in love with love.
I was approaching thirty,
when I proposed to Kee, a recent widow.
When I held my hand
in the lantern flame, she fled,
instructed me not to follow.

Father objected to Margot,
thought her too unstable
to provide sustenance for another.
And Stein, too young.
They were right, of course,
though I would have cared for her,
treated her gently.

I spent several years with Sein,
a prostitute and uneducated, yet
we found a sort of compatibility.
It didn't last. She left
taking both her daughter and the son

who might have been mine.

And, ah, flamboyant Agostina
who might have supported my art
with funds from her thriving cafe.
She was too demanding, I discovered,
for one devoted to painting.

Yellow House

> *In this I can live and breathe,*
> *meditate and paint.*
>
> -VVG

I could tolerate that small hotel no longer!
The disagreeable innkeeper
complained constantly that my equipment
usurped his space, requested I pay more.
I, of course, turned my back,
hissed at him through my teeth.
He argued, red-faced, vehement,
gesticulated violently,
went so far as to seize my property.
I was forced to appeal to a justice-of-the-peace.

I have since located a small house
that rents for just 15 francs;
it is the perfect place — home and studio.
It has two rooms up, two down,
and a bath just next door.
It is *painted the yellow color of fresh butter*
on the outside with glaringly green shutters;
it stands in the full sunlight in a square
which has a green garden with plane trees,
oleanders and acacias.

I call this my *house of light;*
it is quite lovely: whitewashed throughout,
with a red tile floor. And, ah, the sky above it
is so intensely blue. I plan to establish
a commune here where artists gather,
live and work together, share ideas,
expenses, profits. I will invite Monsieur Gauguin.

He will become director of our little group.
He will make bouillabaisse and cassoulets;
perhaps Theo can arrange a small stipend.
I have begun a series of garden paintings
with which to decorate his room.
To save money for frames, I am eating
only bread and eggs. I fill my belly
with innumerable cups of coffee.
My own room will overflow
with paintings of sunflowers.

Vincent's *Sunflowers*

> *Have you seen that portrait Gauguin did of me*
> *painting sunflowers? It was really I, but*
> *it's I gone mad.*
>
> -VVG

Vincent, people whisper,
in his shabby suit. Or, Vincent
in his spattered shirt, sleeves rolled up.
Vincent, his untrimmed ginger hair,
beard a cuckoo's nest.
Smear of umber above his eye —
tongue brush- striped ultramarine.
Do they think I don't hear gossip?

Two years I lived with Theo in Paris,
painted sunflowers while others
painted sidewalk cafés, river boats,
frolicking follies' dancers.
Now, closed in my room in Arles,
I again consider a still life;
unable to afford a meager bouquet,
from the flower seller's stall
I pull a desperate fistful —
roadside sunflowers —
gawky and misunderstood as myself.
Vibrant as the sun. *I'm painting*
with the gusto of a Marseillais
eating bouillabaisse . . .

New pigments extend my spectrum —
paint a lifespan,
brilliant yellow to fading ochre.
Paul will be arriving soon,

and I will make his room bloom
with exuberance.
Nature, like life, is fleeting —
summer comes, summer goes.
I set my easel,
tumble into that sirens' trap: amber,
saffron, ochre, cadmium, gamboge.

Vincent Takes Counsel

> *One must work and dare if one really*
> *wants to live.*
>
> —VVG

Dr. Gachet treats me
with tinctures and herbs,
fears I have absorbed poisons
though rather than grind minerals
I purchase powders,
combine with linseed or poppy oil.
I create a simple layering,
building with oils —
so much depth and vibrancy!

He fusses over mercury
in my vermilion,
fears I will succumb to hatter's madness,
warns of lead in my white,
chrome in my yellows,
even cadmium and arsenic.
He worries; I delight
that I might absorb such color,
become a prism scattering every hue.
What a spectacle I would be then!
More likely, wormwood in my absinthe,
will be my downfall.

Theo's gallery acquires work
by Gauguin, whom I admire.
His talent is large
though I fear it's one part talent,
to two parts pretension,
or perhaps sheer bluster.

He suggested I work
with a camera obscura — a devil's device
that projects the image upon a grid.
Where is the artistry in that!
I did not inquire whether he, himself,
relies on this abomination.
Were I forced to use it,
I would tilt my chin and howl,
rake my nails across the sky.

About My Right Ear

> . . . *keep this object carefully*
>   -VVG

If you are reading this I am dead,
for I gave my word to take our secret to the grave.
There are those who believe I severed my ear
in a fit of melancholia, suicide attempt
over loss of a woman,
a friend,
even dear Theo whom I know
would never abandon me.
These rumors are unfounded;
I offer my unbloodied razor as proof.

No, it was my friend,
the lovely Paul.
He excised that dispensable appendage,
quite without malicious intent,
storming from our lodgings after a row.
I followed.
To apologize? Plead? Curse and hurl insults?
Paul mistook the palette knife I carried
for a razor;
an exceptional swordsman, he struck
a defensive blow.

Remorse was immediate
and profuse,
but fearing police action —
they've little use for painters such as we —
we pledged secrecy.
I wrapped the offending ear,

presented it to Rachael,
a prostitute of whom I occasionally avail myself.
Paul fled to England
neither of us mentioning the incident again.

VVG

Gauguin Tells His Side

> *. . . he can take back his little Martinique canvas*
> *. . . giving me back both my portrait and the two*
> *sunflower canvases which he has taken to Paris.*
>
> -VVG

When I arrived
canvasses covered every surface,
supported every wall; pigments overflowed
an eternally-open paint box.
I was charged with straightening
and handling finances, replenished
time to time by Theo — a gallery clerk.
I felt obliged to help a friend,
acquaintance really, but Theo's pittance
was hardly recompense.
Vincent lacked not just organization
but perception,
never in his life an original idea!
He was producing
nothing worthwhile, but under my tutelage
he produced a series of striking sunflowers —
though he may claim they were done earlier.

Arles is a dreary place: landscape of sameness,
unsophisticated populace. And I
was quite at my wit's end with Vincent —
boisterous one moment, sulky the next.
Our disagreements grew frequent
and heated.
I lasted six weeks.
When he slung a glass of absinthe at me,
I wrote Theo that I could not stay,
then relented

until Vincent again attacked
as I strolled a small park.
It was Christmas Eve. I heard footsteps,
turned, saw Vincent razor in hand.
Realizing I could easily overpower him,
he turned and fled. I checked into a hotel,
slept well for the first time in weeks.
Next morning, I found him in his bed,
missing an ear, bloodied, yet alive.
I left for Paris.

Gabrielle Clarifies The Matter

> *It is only too true that a lot of artists are mentally ill -*
> *it's a life which, to put it mildly, makes one an outsider.*
>
> -VVG

Folks is wrong 'bout me an' Monsieur Vincent!
It ain't like they say. He's kinda funny lookin'
with skinny legs an' orange hair.
He's kinda sad too, but he's a nice man.
He give me three sous to fetch roasted chestnuts
an' a bottle of absinthe. He'd pay to paint me too,
but Madame says that ain't proper.

I were jus' a farm kid, milkin' Old Anny
when the biggest, hairiest dog I ever seen,
jumped on me
growlin' an' bitin' sumpin' fierce.
Papa reckons he was some kinda Irish wolf.

He carried me to a doctor in Paris
what give me nasty-tastin' medicine,
bled me with slimy black leeches,
an' rubbed on stinky green salve
that burned real bad.
Papa didn' have money, so I work —
Papa says I'm old enough.
I clean an' fetch, change beds, wash sheets.
Folks whisper I'm a fallen woman
cause I work here. That ain't true!
I ain't any kind of woman, yet. Papa says
when I am, I'll work somewheres else.

I don' know why Monsieur Vincent

give me his ear.
I thought maybe it were a sweetie
or a pretty shell. When I unwrapped it
I screamed an' screamed.

Self-Portrait with Bandage ~ 1889

> *I am seeking, I am striving, I am in it*
> *with all my heart.*
>
> -VVG

Recently, I've observed Death watching
from the shadow, chair beside my bed,
window of a passing carriage —
a gauzy figure at vision's edge.
His is not a fearsome countenance,
coat crumpled and frayed as my own,
footwear scuffed,
and the hand he extends is calloused,
steady, comforting.

I consider asking him to pose,
but sensing my intent he shakes his head,
so, I resort to painting myself
as I have so often before
with various accoutrements:
pipe, hat, bandage.
I use the Impressionists' loose brushstrokes,
but retain heavy outlines
adapted from Japanese woodblocks.
My hands tremble and vision dims;
I fear this portrait may be my last.

Starry Night ~ 1889

> *. . . night with cypresses*
> *or — perhaps above a field of ripe wheat. . .*
> -VVG

I am not allowed to paint in my room
though I sketch with ink and charcoal:
rolling foothills
run diagonally across the canvas,
wheat field, and cypresses.
I've painted this scene twenty times:
sunrise, moonrise, midday, overcast,
windy, even once in rain,
but I'd yet to paint cypresses as I see them,
flame shaped
and a difficult shade of bottle green.

This time, I paint swirling mistral winds
like those that trigger my melancholy.
Lighter shades of blue along the horizon
suggest coming dawn, but this is a night scene,
one I might see from my window.
I do take liberties: include St. Remy
though it is not visible and the steeple
is reminiscent of the north.
I've remodeled the gibbous moon
to a crescent, its blurred aureole
barely showing through.

I am displeased with this effort,
and though I was to send seven works to Theo
I have found postage exorbitant
and will pull three — including this one.
Except for Aries, it is accurate

though I've oversized its stars.
My hope lies in stars;
after death
perhaps I can exist among them
in another plane.

Theo Speaks of Vincent

I loved him,
as I'd love a scarred alley cat
or broken-winged pigeon,
a blend of love and pity.
His raging passion,
deep despair, and self-loathing.
I warned him
from that whore who would
palm off her bastard as his son,
settled him in Arles.
Johanna loved him too;
we set up shows, encouraged,
found buyers, sent Paul
to care for him, a grave error.
How could we expect such egos
to exist in harmony?
Then, the incident with the ear.

After the gunshot — I rushed bedside.
Bandaged, wan, smoking his pipe,
he pushed blankets to his waist,
assured me he was fine.
Three days later he was dead,
world far too sullied for his honesty,
too calloused for his constancy.

Dr. Gachet Remembers

> *. . . crying so much that he*
> *could only stammer a very confused farewell*
> *(the most beautiful way, perhaps).*
>   -Émile Bernard

Yes, I knew Vincent as both patient
and friend. We were alike, he and I,
gaunt, scrawny, given to melancholy.
His began at an early age;
his certainties, impulses,
and passions never fit in anywhere.

His brother, Theo, contacted me,
thought I could counsel, could help.
And we found rapport, Vincent and I.
I provided a retreat, sanctuary,
protection from those who'd criticize,
snigger, jeer.

He lived too much inside his head
where skies were mandarin and madder,
cinnabar and saffron, marigold and quince.
The way he saw color! I hear him now,
raving about the sky, the sky!
How I envied his passion,
standing stoop shouldered beneath
the weight of stars —
blazing cartwheels in deep purple night.

I never understood about the ear;
perhaps he wished to silence criticism.
I would have predicted
he'd more likely sever fingers,

as though they'd let him down.
He was a perfectionist, you know.
And the suicide. He gave no indication . . .

Where do you suppose he procured
a gun? I would not have expected him
to own one.

Vincent's Mother Speaks

                                        -VVG

He blamed me, you know,
naming him after his dead brother.
As if Vincent weren't
a common enough name,
as if a thousand others didn't carry it.
He was always difficult,
vehement, contentious,
never kept a job.
He grew obsessed with Catholicism,
then the Belgian Church,
but it never came to anything.
His plans never came to anything.
And his infatuations, impossible!
Let him meet any troubled woman,
and he'd pledge undying love,
descend into melancholia when she ran,
terrified and overwhelmed.
I'll tell you, it exhausted even me
to be around him;
He took up with that whore,
spoke of her son as his own.
Father warned him;
even Theo, overindulgent Theo,
threatened to cut funds.
But, did he listen? Did he ever listen?
I was relieved when he moved out
and when Theo settled him in Arles.
But what fool severs his own ear?

I wrote Theo then, saying
it would be best if Our Lord took him.
All those canvases he had us store,
quite filling the attic!
After his death — suicide of all things —
I carted them off to the dump.
Such pitiable efforts — perspective off,
paint applied with a trowel!
I'm the artist in this family.
Theo's wife, poor deluded woman,
tried to gather every canvas,
for a show she said,
as if any gallery would display such rubbish.

Vincent Speaks from the Grave

> *I wish to take my revenge by doing brilliant color,*
> *well arranged, resplendent.*

-VVG

They dismissed me as mad,
and though likely right, it's irrelevant.
Why do they insist it be a malady?
Can it not be splendor
of natural light? Luminescence
of sun? Critics say I ingested
heavy metals. Ate paint.
Suffered epilepsy. Alcoholism.
Syphilis. Paranoid-schizophrenia.

Puny explanations!
Nor did Dr. Gachet poison me
with digitalis,
cause me to see auras,
the world through a yellow lens.

Mother, ultimate betrayer,
tossed my work,
I could have expected no less
from a mediocre talent
outshined by a son
she disparaged and despised.

Now I am vindicated!
Buyers cherish my paintings
as holy relics, finger bones of a saint,
bit of the true cross.
Does madness exclude genius?

The line between them, I've heard,
is fine.

ÉMILE BERNARD SPEAKS OF VINCENT'S FUNERAL

On the walls of the room where his body was laid out all his last canvases were hung making a sort of halo for him and the brilliance of the genius that radiated from them made this death even more painful for us artists who were there. The coffin was covered with a simple white cloth and surrounded with masses of flowers, the sunflowers he loved so much, yellow dahlias, yellow flowers everywhere. It was, you will remember, his favorite color, the symbol of the light that he dreamed of as being in the people's hearts as well as in works of art.

Near him also on the floor in front of his coffin were his easel, his folding stool and his brushes . . .

At three o'clock the body was moved, friends of his carrying it to the hearse, a number of people in the company were in tears. Theodore Van Gogh who was devoted to his brother, who had always supported him in his struggle to support himself from his art was sobbing pitifully the whole time . . .

The sun was terribly hot outside. We climbed the hill outside Auvers talking about him, about the daring impulse he had given to art, of the great projects he was always thinking about, and of the good he had done to all of us.

We reached the cemetery, a small new cemetery strewn with new tombstones. It is on the little hill above the fields that were ripe for harvest under a wide blue sky he would still have loved

. . . perhaps.

Then he was lowered into the grave . . .

Anyone would have started crying at that moment . . . the day was too much made for him for one not to imagine that he was still alive and enjoying it . . .

Source:
Emile Bernard. Letter to Albert Aurier. Written 2 August 1889 in Paris. Translated by Robert Harrison, edited by Robert Harrison, number. URL: http://www.webexhibits. org/vangogh/letter/21/etc-Bernard-Aurier.htm

ACKNOWLEDGMENTS

"About My Right Ear" was originally published in *The Homestead Review*

"*Congregation Leaving the Reformed Church in Nuenen ~ 1884-5*" was originally published in *The Homestead Review*

"Dr. Gachet Remembers" was originally published in *New Plains Review*

"*Portrait of Dr. Gachet ~ 1890*" was originally published in *The Homestead Review*

"*The Potato Eaters ~ 1885*" was originally published in *The Homestead Review*

"*Self Portrait with Bandage*" was originally published in *Panoply*

"*Starry Night ~ 1889*" was originally published in *Slant*

"Theo Speaks of Vincent" was originally published in *The Homestead Review*

"Van Gogh's *Sunflowers*" was originally published in *Panoply*

"Vincent Dreams *Irises*" was originally published in *The Poeming Pigeon*

"Vincent in Love" was originally published in *Panoply*

"Vincent Paints a Self-Portrait" was originally published in *Panoply*

"Vincent Speaks of Theo" was originally published in *Dime Show Review*

"Yellow House" was originally published in *Mojave River Review*

Ann Howells edited *Illya's Honey for* seventeen years, first in print and then four years online. Named a "Distinguished Poet of Dallas" by the city in 2001, she has received seven Pushcart nominations and taken first place in several local/state competitions. She served as President of Dallas Poets Community (501-c-3) for four years and as Treasurer for many more. She also serves on advisory boards and panels, judges poetry competitions, participates in taking poetry into schools—elementary through college—and presents her work at festivals and conferences. Over 600 of her poems have appeared in small press and university publications in the United States and Europe—including *Spillway, THEMA, Little Patuxent Review, Magma* (England) and *Crannog* (Ireland).

facebook.com/AnnHowellsDPC

ALSO BY ANN HOWELLS

Books

So Long As We Speak Their Names
(Kelsay Press, 2019)

Under a Lone Star
Illustrated by Dallas artist, J. Darrell Kirkley
(Village Books Press, 2016),

Cattlemen & Cadillacs, an anthology of D/FW poets
(Editor, Dallas Poets Community Press, 2016)

Chapbooks

Softly Beating Wings
Winner of the William D. Barney Contest
(Blackbead Books, 2017)

Letters for My Daughter
(Flutter Press, 2016)

the Rosebud Diaries
(Willets Press, 2012 —limited edition)

Black Crow in Flight
(Editor's Choice, Main Street Rag Publishing, 2007)

www.ingramcontent.com/pod-product-compliance
Lightning Source LLC
Chambersburg PA
CBHW021345060726
47591CB00006B/2171